Soccer Superstars

By James Buckley, Jr.

The
Child's
World®

www.childsworld.com

J
796.33
BUC

Published in the United States of America by The Child's World®
P.O. Box 326 • Chanhassen, MN 55317-0326
800-599-READ • www.childsworld.com

ACKNOWLEDGMENTS

The Child's World®: Mary Berendes, Publishing Director

Produced by Shoreline Publishing Group LLC
President / Editorial Director: James Buckley, Jr.
Designer: Tom Carling, carlingdesign.com
Cover Art: Slimfilms
Copy Editor: Beth Adelman

Photo Credits
Cover—Zidane/Beckham: Action Plus Sports Images; Donovan/Adu:
AP/Wide World.
Interior—Action Plus Sports Images: 1, 3, 4, 6, 7, 9, 13, 14, 15, 17, 18, 19,
20, 21, 23, 25; AP/Wide World: 26, 28, 29; Alfredo Estrella/Getty
Images: 10; Vanina Lucchesi/Getty Images: 8.

LIBRARY OF CONGRESS CATALOGING-IN-PUBLICATION DATA

Buckley, James, 1963-
  Soccer superstars / by James Buckley, Jr.
     p. cm. — (Boys rock!)
  Includes bibliographical references and index.
  ISBN 1-59296-736-1 (library bound : alk. paper)
  1. Soccer players—Biography—Juvenile literature. I. Title. II. Series.
  GV942.7.A1B83 2006
  796.334092'2—dc22
                              2006001652

CONTENTS

WORLD Champs!

Soccer is the world's most popular sport. Billions of people all over the world root for their favorite teams.

The world's best soccer players play for two teams. They play for their national teams. They also play in pro leagues, often outside of their home country.

The World Cup

The goal for every national team is to win the **World Cup** (right). This competition is held every four years. In 2002, Brazil won its fifth World Cup. A new champ will be crowned in 2006.

Some of the world's most exciting soccer players come from Brazil.

In recent years, the best Brazilian player has been Ronaldo, a three-time World Player of the Year. In 2002, he helped Brazil win the World Cup. He had eight goals and won the Golden Boot award as high scorer. Ronaldo also plays for the pro team Real (ray-AHL) Madrid in Spain.

Most players from Brazil go by just one name. This is Ronaldo.

The powerful **forward** Ronaldinho was the 2004 World Player of the Year. Tall and fast, this young star is excellent at using his **head**.

We don't mean his brain! In soccer, you can hit the ball with your head.

Ronaldinho (roh-nahl-DEE-nyoh) shows off perfect form for a pass.

Ronaldinho plays for the pro team FC Barcelona, another team in Spain.

In that Spanish league, the two Brazilian scoring stars, Ronaldo and Ronaldinho, must play against fellow Brazilian Roberto Carlos. This short but powerful lefty is a top **defender**.

The Best Ever?

Many people call former Brazil star Pelé (PAY-lay) the best soccer player of all time. He helped his country win three World Cups. He scored 1,281 goals in his long career (1957–1979).

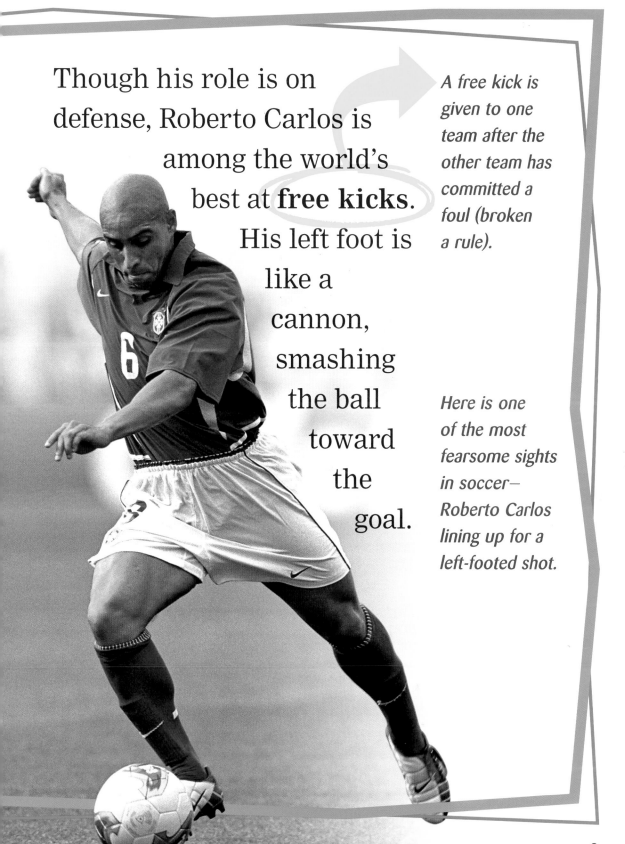

Though his role is on defense, Roberto Carlos is among the world's best at **free kicks**. His left foot is like a cannon, smashing the ball toward the goal.

A free kick is given to one team after the other team has committed a foul (broken a rule).

Here is one of the most fearsome sights in soccer— Roberto Carlos lining up for a left-footed shot.

With all the goals he scores, Mexico's Jared Borgetti gets plenty of chances to celebrate!

Argentina won World Cup championships in 1978 and 1986.

Brazil is one of many soccer-loving countries in South America. Argentina, for example, has won two World Cups and produced many great players. They include forward Diego Maradona, who retired in 1991.

The top players on today's Argentina team are speedy forward Hernán Crespo and top scorer Roberto Ayala.

Though not in South America, another soccer-loving, Spanish-speaking nation is Mexico. Mexico is a powerful **rival** of its neighbor, the United States. The top player for Mexico's *Tricolores* ("three colors," from their flag) team is Jared Borgetti. He scored 14 goals while helping Mexico earn a spot in the 2006 World Cup tournament.

A rival in sports is a team or player that you play often, usually in very emotional games.

2

SUPERSTARS OF Europe

Soccer was first played in Europe about 150 years ago. Today, that **continent** is home to some of the world's best players.

In 2002, Zinnedine Zidane led France to the World Cup championship. Zidane is an expert at passing. He makes such awesome passes, sometimes it seems as if he has eyes in the back of his head.

Getting air! Zinnedine Zidane leaps to avoid a sliding tackle.

Heads up! Michael Ballack battles for a ball in the air. As a midfielder, he plays both offense and defense.

The German national team is led by **midfielder** Michael Ballack. His pro team is Bayern Munich. He has been named the German league's top player three times.

In Italy, soccer is by far the most popular sport in the country.

Several of the world's best players come from Italy. One of them, Paolo Maldini, helped the Italian national team play in four World Cups.

Italian star Paolo Maldini shows off his cool national team warm-up jacket.

A **fullback**, he is probably the best defensive player in the world.

The first pro soccer teams played in England in the 1840s. The top league in England today, the **Premier** League, features some amazing players.

Forward Michael Owen burst onto the world soccer scene in 1998. Even though he was only 17, he scored a memorable goal in the World Cup against Argentina.

Owen later helped his pro team Liverpool win three important titles. His scoring skills have made him a star.

Another top scorer is forward Wayne Rooney. He scored a goal for England when he was even younger than Owen! A speedy, burly player, Rooney will be a star for years to come.

Gooaalll! England's Wayne Rooney leaps over a goalie after scoring.

England's David Beckham is perhaps the most famous soccer player in the world. He plays for Real Madrid.

"Becks" shows off his great kicking form.

School Boy!

David Beckham is trying to use his worldwide fame to spread soccer to the United States. In 2005, he thrilled his fans when he opened a special soccer school in Los Angeles.

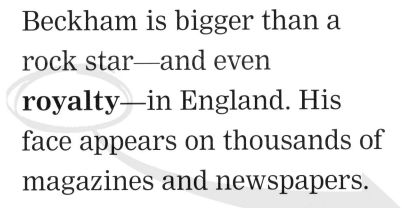

Beckham is bigger than a rock star—and even **royalty**—in England. His face appears on thousands of magazines and newspapers.

Royalty are the kings and queens of a country and their families.

On the field, he's a top-flight midfielder. His ability to make pinpoint, curving passes and free kicks have made him a star!

One of the most important skills in soccer is **dribbling**. This doesn't mean spilling a drink—it means controlling the ball with short taps by each foot.

Luís Figo (in his red Portugal jersey) dribbles past David Beckham.

Portugal's Luís Figo is one of the world's best dribblers. After starring for Real Madrid for years, he joined the Italian pro team Inter Milan in 2005.

The large nation of Ukraine in eastern Europe is home to high-scoring **striker**, or forward, Andriy Shevchenko.

In 2003, the man they call "Shev" was named Europe's top player. In 2004, he helped his pro team, Italy's A.C. Milan, win an important championship. He remains a feared scoring threat for Ukraine, too.

3

A BIG WORLD OF Soccer

So far, every World Cup champion has come from Europe or South America. Other areas of the world, however, are growing in soccer success.

Soccer is quickly increasing in popularity in Asian countries. Millions of people play the game in China. Japan recently started a hot new pro league.

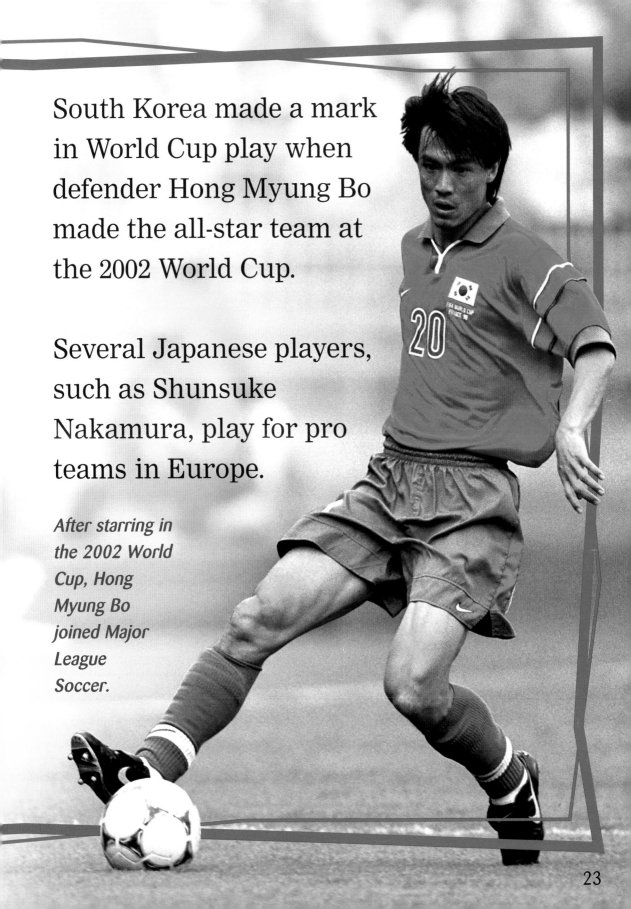

South Korea made a mark in World Cup play when defender Hong Myung Bo made the all-star team at the 2002 World Cup.

Several Japanese players, such as Shunsuke Nakamura, play for pro teams in Europe.

After starring in the 2002 World Cup, Hong Myung Bo joined Major League Soccer.

Another area of the soccer world that is booming is Africa. The continent features many young, exciting players who are making their mark in pro leagues around the world.

France was a World Cup champion in 1998, but Drogba was not yet on the team.

Samuel Eto'o (eh-TOH-oh) is from Cameroon, but he plays pro soccer with FC Barcelona in Spain. He was named Africa's top player in 2003 and 2004.

Didier Drogba is another African star. He is from the nation of Côte d'Ivoire.

Samuel Eto'o is known for his amazing goals.

He grew up in France, however, where he learned his soccer skills. Drogba is now one of the top scorers in the English League.

Meanwhile, Americans only love baseball, football, and basketball, right? Wrong! More American kids play soccer than any other sport. Plus, many people come to the United States from other countries. They bring their love of soccer with them to their new home.

One of the players they can all cheer for is U.S. goalkeeper Kasey Keller. This tall, strong, shot-stopper is one of the best "keepers" in the world. Kasey has played for the U.S. in three World Cups. He's played pro soccer in England, and he also plays for a pro team in Germany.

U.S. Pro Soccer

In 1995, Major League Soccer (MLS), a new pro soccer league, started in the United States. Ten years later, it was still going strong, with 12 teams. Many of the top players on the U.S. national team play in MLS.

Landon Donovan has become one of the world's top strikers.

In his first game with the U.S. National Team in 2000, Landon Donovan scored a goal against rival Mexico. He hasn't stopped scoring since.

Landon's nose for the goal has made him America's top soccer star. He has been the National Player of the Year three times. He plays in the MLS for Los Angeles.

Another young man—and we do mean young—is ready to join Landon on the U.S. team. Freddy Adu turned pro when he was only 15! A native of Ghana who became a U.S. citizen, Freddy has speed and scoring skills.

Freddy and all the U.S. players have their eye on making sure the United States makes its mark on the soccer stage.

Fifteen? Really? Yes, it's true. Freddy Adu became a pro soccer star when he joined D.C. United at age 15.

GLOSSARY

continent   one of Earth's seven large land areas

defender   in soccer, someone who plays in front of the goal, helping to keep the other team from scoring (sometimes called a **fullback**)

dribbling   advancing the ball by tapping it with the feet

forward   in soccer, a person who plays closest to the other team's goal and often scores goals (also called a **striker**)

free kick   a kick given to a team after a foul has been committed against one of its players

head   in soccer, to hit the ball with your forehead for a pass or a shot

midfielder   position between forwards and defenders

premier   the first or the best—also the name of England's top soccer league, the Premier League

rival   somebody competing for the same thing—also a sports team another team plays often and really wants to defeat

royalty   in countries that have a king or queen, members of the ruling family

World Cup   soccer's international championship, held every four years in a different place

FIND OUT MORE

BOOKS

The Everything Kids Soccer Book
by Deborah Crisfield (Adams Media, Avon, MA) 2002
Rules, history, playing tips, games, trivia, and lots more are in this fun-filled book.

Eyewitness Soccer
by Hugh Hornby (DK Publishing, New York) 2000
This book, part of a popular series of illustrated books, features the gear, souvenirs, history, and rules of soccer.

Soccer: A History of the World's Most Popular Sport
by Mark Stewart (Franklin Watts, New York) 1998
From soccer's early days to today's World Cup stars, this book traces the story of how soccer conquered the world!

Soccer Cats: Kick It!
by Matt Christopher (Little Brown, New York) 2003
The famous sports writer tackles soccer in this fictional story of a young team.

WEB SITES

Visit our home page for lots of links about world soccer teams and players: www.childsworld.com/links

Note to Parents, Teachers, and Librarians: We routinely check our Web links to make sure they're safe, active sites—so encourage your readers to check them out!

INDEX

JAMES BUCKLEY, JR., has written more than 45 books for young readers on sports, history, and pop culture. He also has a long soccer background. He has played since he was a kid and still plays goalie in an amateur league. He has also coached youth soccer (his latest team is the Purple Wizards).